DATE DUE

·VISUAL GUIDES·
FLYING MACHINES

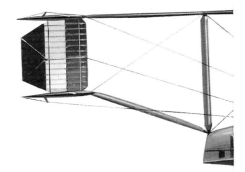

FR
New York • Chic

© 1994 Franklin Watts

Franklin Watts
95 Madison Avenue
New York, NY 10016

Library of Congress
Cataloging-in-Publication Data
Barrett, Norman S.
    Flying machines / Norman
Barrett.
        p. cm. – (Visual guides)
    Includes index.
    ISBN 0-531-14301-5
    1. Airplanes – Juvenile
literature.   [1. Airplanes.]
    I. Title.
    II. Series: Barrett, Norman S.
Visual guides.
    TL547.B374   1994
    629.133 – dc20   93-33238
                        CIP   AC

A number of the illustrations in
this book, which appeared
originally in titles from the
Wings, First Look and Spotlight
series, are based on material
created by David Jefferis.

Printed in Hong Kong

Series Editor
Norman Barrett

Designed by
K and Co

Picture Research by
Ruth Sonntag

Photographs by
Norman Barrett
Bell Helicopter Textron
British Aerospace
British Airways
Cameron Balloons
French Government Tourist Office
NASA
Thunder & Colt
US Navy
Westland Helicopters

New Illustrations by
Rhoda and Robert Burns

Contents

Airliner

More people have flown on airliners than on any other flying machines. The airliner is the fastest form of travel for the general public. People use airliners for both holiday and business travel. There are airports in most countries of the world.

Airliners range in size from small propeller-driven planes used for short journeys to jumbo jets that carry as many as 500 passengers between continents.

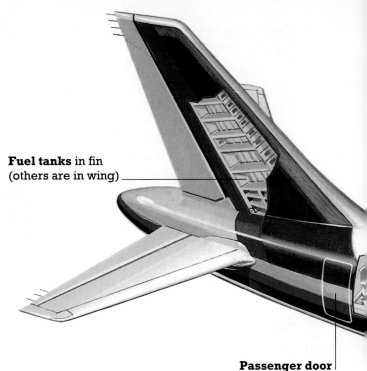

Fuel tanks in fin (others are in wing)

Passenger door

Rest room

◁ The Airbus A320 is a modern jetliner built by a group of European manufacturers. It contains the latest in technical advances. In the cockpit instrument panel, gauges and dials have been replaced by computer-controlled TV screens.

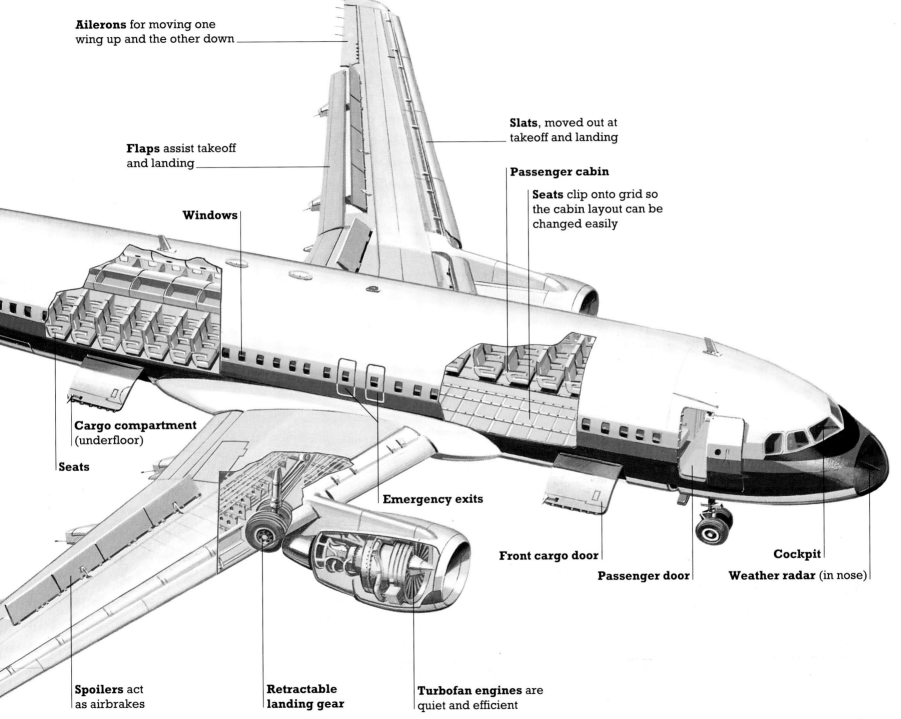

Ailerons for moving one wing up and the other down

Flaps assist takeoff and landing

Slats, moved out at takeoff and landing

Passenger cabin

Seats clip onto grid so the cabin layout can be changed easily

Windows

Cargo compartment (underfloor)

Seats

Emergency exits

Front cargo door

Cockpit

Passenger door

Weather radar (in nose)

Spoilers act as airbrakes

Retractable landing gear

Turbofan engines are quiet and efficient

Preparing an airliner

Before every flight, there is great activity around an airliner as ground staff carry out their work. Mechanics check the engines, tires, and brakes and any other items that might have been reported by the previous flight deck and cabin crews.

Different groups of workers refuel the airliner, load cargo and baggage, clean the cabins and restrooms, and take fresh food and drink aboard for the passengers.

▽ Airliners may be serviced with the help of special scissor trucks. These are raised to the height of the cabin door.

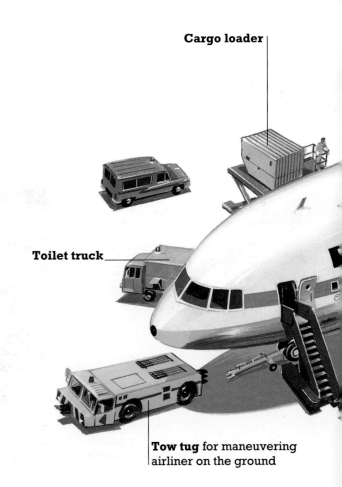

Fuel tanker

Cargo loader

Toilet truck

Tow tug for maneuvering airliner on the ground

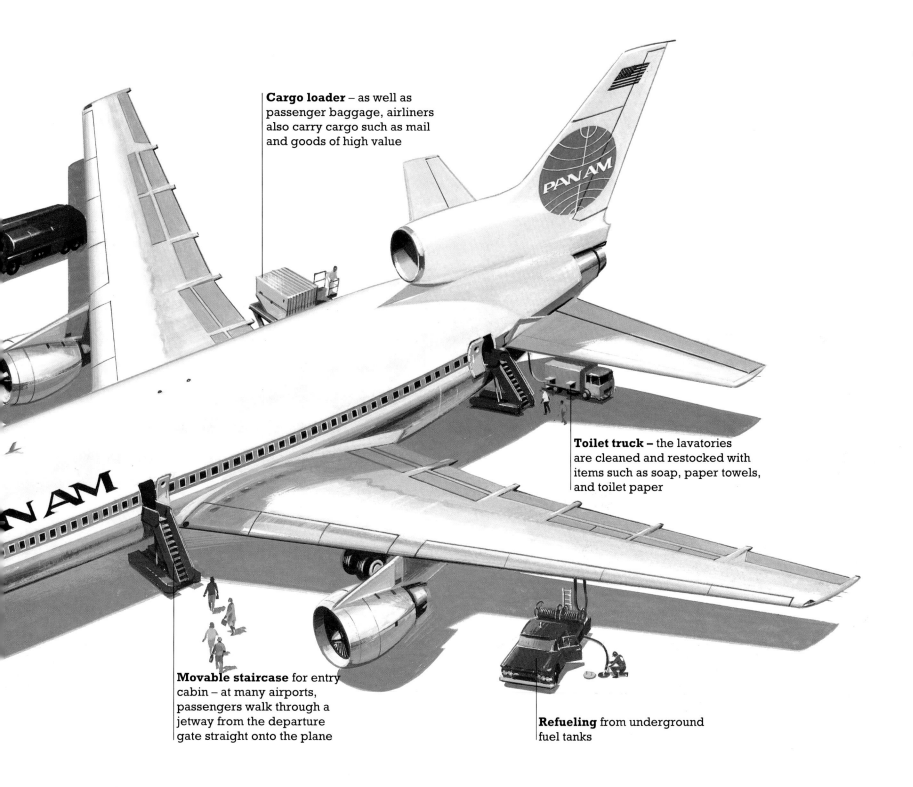

Cargo loader – as well as passenger baggage, airliners also carry cargo such as mail and goods of high value

Toilet truck – the lavatories are cleaned and restocked with items such as soap, paper towels, and toilet paper

Movable staircase for entry cabin – at many airports, passengers walk through a jetway from the departure gate straight onto the plane

Refueling from underground fuel tanks

Concorde

Concorde is the world's first supersonic passenger airliner. It flies at 1,482 mph (2,385 kmph), twice the speed of sound (Mach 2), and delivers people to their destination in little more than half the time taken by other jetliners.

Britain and France cooperated in the design of Concorde. It can carry 128 passengers and has a range of 3,915 miles (6,300 km). The first Concorde went into service in 1976.

▽ The supersonic Concorde can reach speeds faster than a bullet from a gun. Only 14 Concordes have entered service. Their main routes are between Europe and the United States.

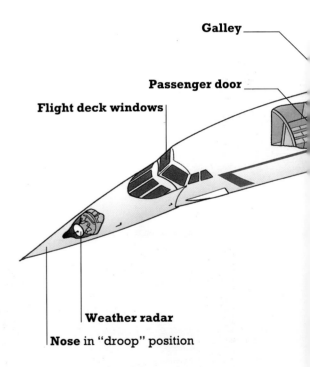

Galley

Passenger door

Flight deck windows

Weather radar

Nose in "droop" position

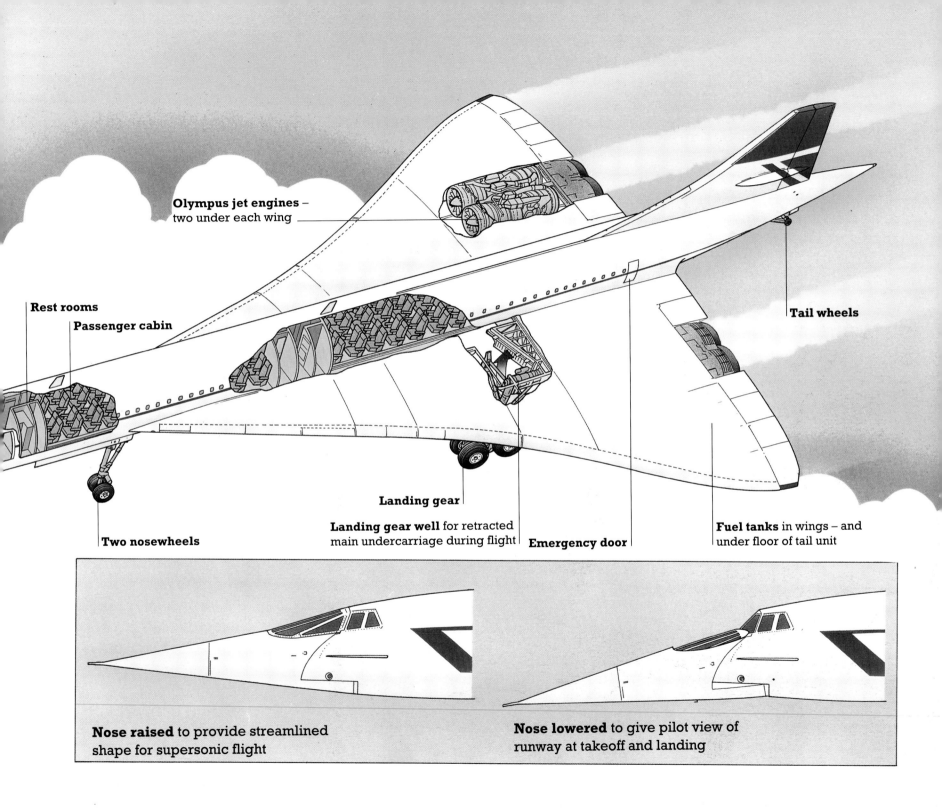

Olympus jet engines – two under each wing

Rest rooms

Passenger cabin

Tail wheels

Two nosewheels

Landing gear

Landing gear well for retracted main undercarriage during flight

Emergency door

Fuel tanks in wings – and under floor of tail unit

Nose raised to provide streamlined shape for supersonic flight

Nose lowered to give pilot view of runway at takeoff and landing

◁ HOTOL (HOrizontal TakeOff and Landing) is an advanced British design for a space plane. This computer-controlled craft would take off from an ordinary runway like an airliner, fly into space, then fly back again for a normal landing. The idea is to reduce the cost of rocket launches to place satellites in orbit. The next step would be an orbital airliner, carrying people in a low orbit round the earth.

Future supersonics

Any future supersonic airliner will have to carry more passengers than Concorde and have a longer range. Manufacturers are studying ideas for a 300-passenger airliner able to cruise at Mach 5. One such design, the Machliner, is shown opposite.

Looking further into the future, a space plane would fly to and from orbit in space like a normal aircraft. HOTOL, an advanced design, is also shown opposite.

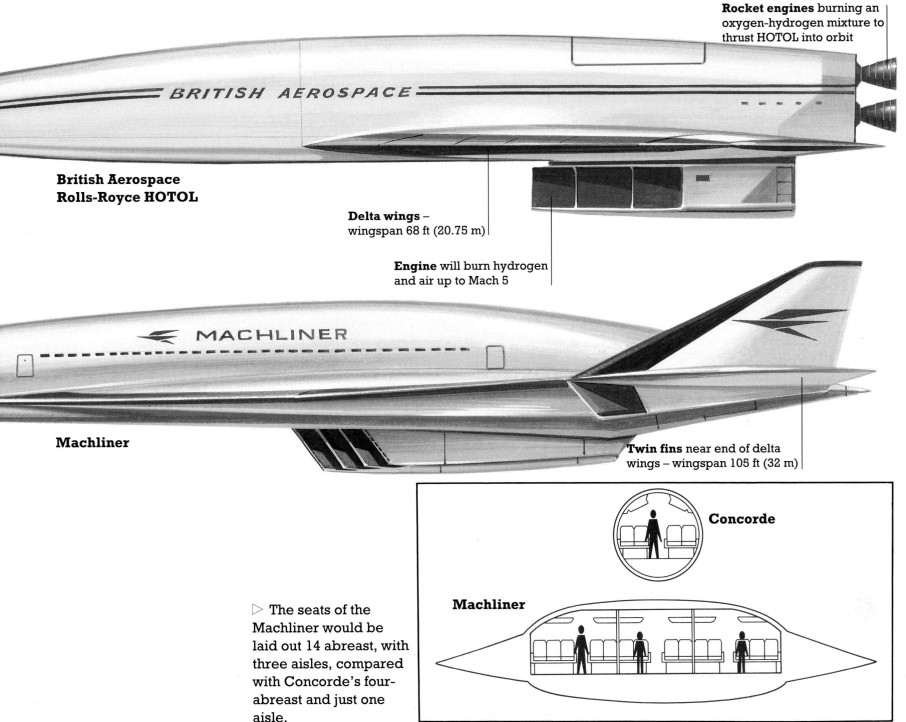

Rocket engines burning an oxygen-hydrogen mixture to thrust HOTOL into orbit

British Aerospace Rolls-Royce HOTOL

Delta wings – wingspan 68 ft (20.75 m)

Engine will burn hydrogen and air up to Mach 5

Machliner

Twin fins near end of delta wings – wingspan 105 ft (32 m)

Concorde

Machliner

▷ The seats of the Machliner would be laid out 14 abreast, with three aisles, compared with Concorde's four-abreast and just one aisle.

Airliner progress

Airliners have become faster and larger since the first passenger service opened in 1914 in Florida. The tiny Benoist flying boat was 26 feet (7.92 m) long and carried one passenger. Today's jumbo jets, the Boeing 747s, measure 231 feet 10 inches (70.66 m) and carry as many as 500 passengers. The airliners pictured here are drawn to scale.

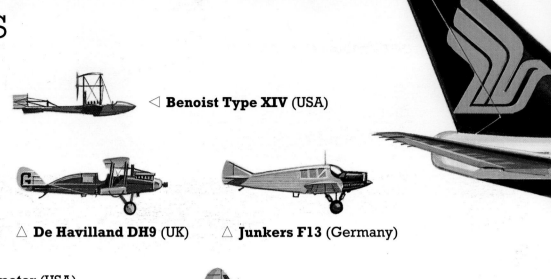

◁ **Benoist Type XIV** (USA)

△ **De Havilland DH9** (UK)

△ **Junkers F13** (Germany)

◁ **Ford Tri-motor** (USA)

△ **Boeing 247** (USA)

△ **Handley Page HP42E** (UK)

▽ **Douglas DC-3** (USA)

▽ **Boeing 707-320** (USA)

△ **Short C-class Empire boat** (UK)

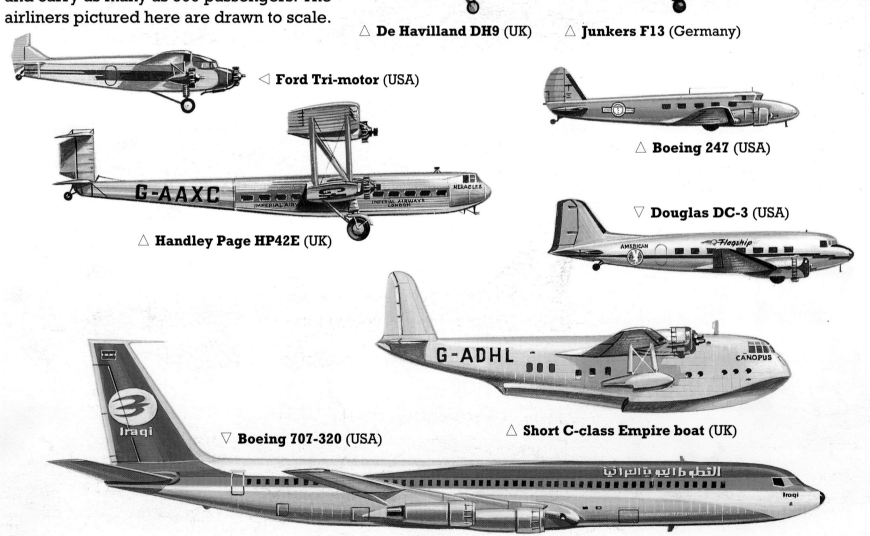

▷ **De Havilland Comet 1** (UK)

△ **Boeing 747-300** (USA)

△ **Aerospatiale/BAC Concorde** (France/UK)

▷ **Airbus A320** (European consortium)

▽ **McDonnell Douglas MD-11** (USA)

Airline markings

There are more than 500 airlines in the world. Each airline has its own markings, which are painted on the body and tail of all their aircraft.

The aircraft markings illustrated on these pages represent airlines from all parts of the world.

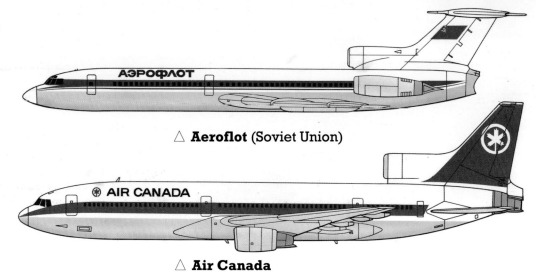

△ **Aeroflot** (Soviet Union)

△ **Air Canada**

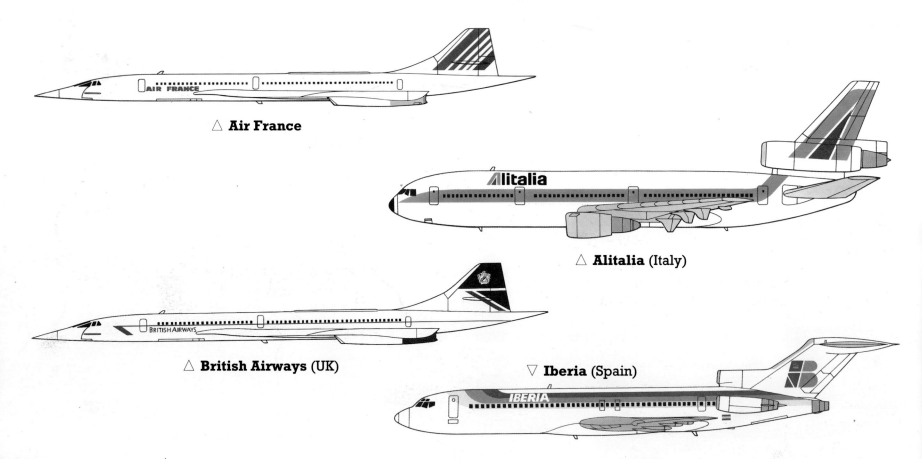

△ **Air France**

△ **Alitalia** (Italy)

△ **British Airways** (UK)

▽ **Iberia** (Spain)

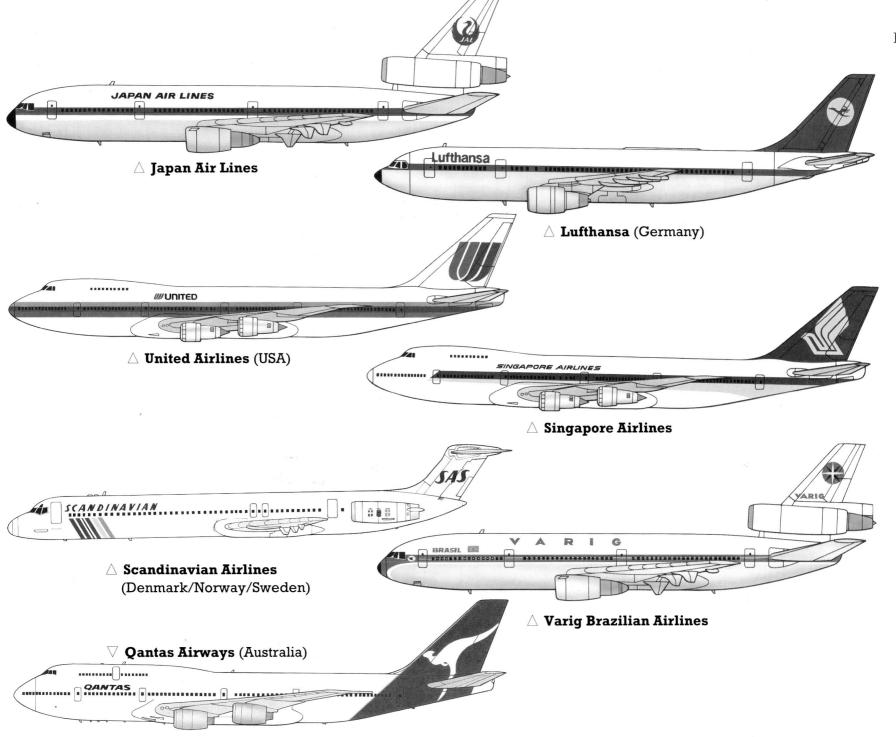

△ **Japan Air Lines**

△ **Lufthansa** (Germany)

△ **United Airlines** (USA)

△ **Singapore Airlines**

△ **Scandinavian Airlines**
(Denmark/Norway/Sweden)

△ **Varig Brazilian Airlines**

▽ **Qantas Airways** (Australia)

▽ A modern seaplane. Whereas a flying boat floats on its hull, seaplanes have large floats. Most seaplanes are small aircraft used for carrying passengers to and from offshore islands or between islands.

▽ In the 1930s, the Empire boats of Imperial Airways gave passengers standards of comfort that have never been bettered. The passengers sat in large armchairs, there was a promenade deck, and fresh food was prepared for each meal.

Retractable antenna for direction finding and "homing"

Radio operator

Masthead light

Flight deck

Captain (right) and **first officer**

Mooring hatch

Mooring equipment

Gangway to upper deck

Landing light (retracted)

Mail compartments – the aircraft carried more than a ton of mail plus baggage

Flight clerk

Flying boat

Flying boats take off and land on the sea. The golden age of flying boats was the 1930s, when they moored at harbors around the world.

The unlimited takeoff length of the open water meant that flying boats could be made bigger than land-based planes. This allowed them to carry fuel for long-distance flights and gave them lots of space for passengers.

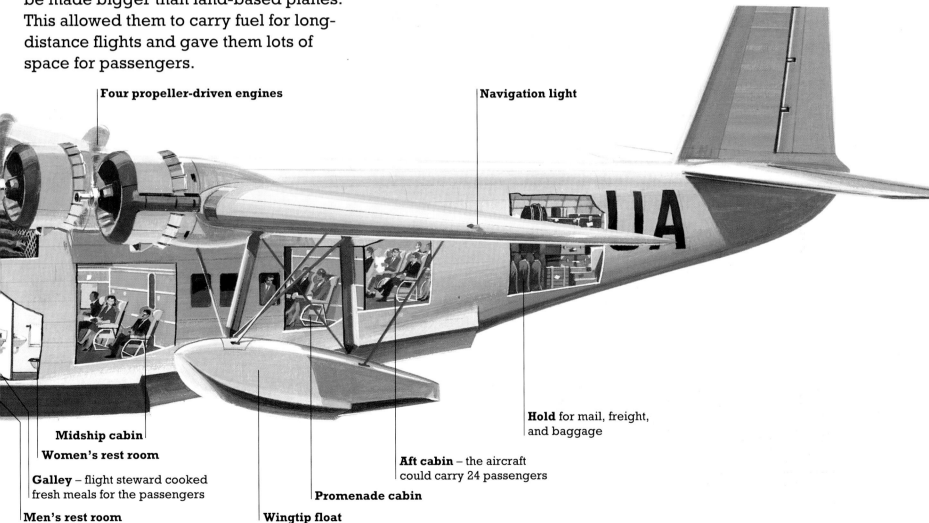

Four propeller-driven engines

Navigation light

Hold for mail, freight, and baggage

Midship cabin

Women's rest room

Galley – flight steward cooked fresh meals for the passengers

Aft cabin – the aircraft could carry 24 passengers

Promenade cabin

Men's rest room

Wingtip float

Helicopter

Helicopters perform tasks that other aircraft cannot do. Their ability to take off and land straight up and down and to hover motionless in the air makes them suitable for rescue work and other specialized jobs.

Helicopters have moving wings called rotors. These have several blades. Most helicopters have a large rotor to power the craft, and a small rotor at the back to stop it from spinning out of control. Some helicopters have two main rotors.

▽ The Westland Sea King is a British-made version of the American Sikorsky S-61. It is an all-around helicopter, used widely for search-and-rescue work by navies and air forces. It is also used for carrying troops, casualty evacuation, and attacking submarines.

Engines – the Sea King has two powerful engines and can fly on one if the other fails

Navigation light

Flight deck

Hull – boat-shaped for landing on water in an emergency

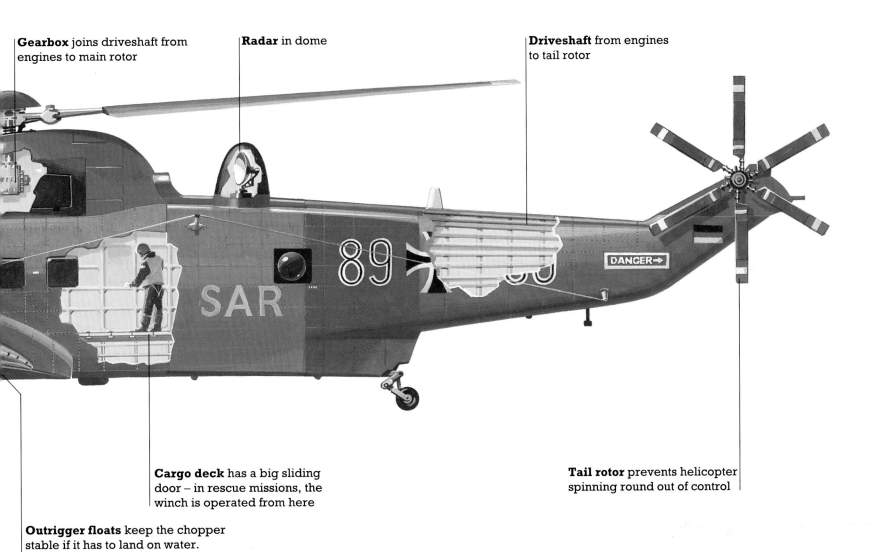

Gearbox joins driveshaft from engines to main rotor

Radar in dome

Driveshaft from engines to tail rotor

89

SAR

DANGER➡

Cargo deck has a big sliding door – in rescue missions, the winch is operated from here

Tail rotor prevents helicopter spinning round out of control

Outrigger floats keep the chopper stable if it has to land on water. The floats also house the main landing gear

Advanced helicopter

The EH 101 is a new design from EH Industries, a joint British/Italian company. Built with the latest lightweight materials, the EH 101 will have speed, considerable lifting power, and unequaled safety features.

The same basic airframe is designed to produce three versions – for civilian (pictured below), naval (illustrated right), and army use.

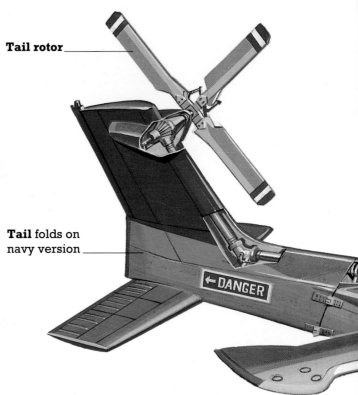

Tail rotor

Tail folds on navy version

← DANGER

◁ The EH 101 during trials. It can cruise at 184 mph (296 km/h) – 21 mph (33 km/h) faster than other helicopters of a similar size.

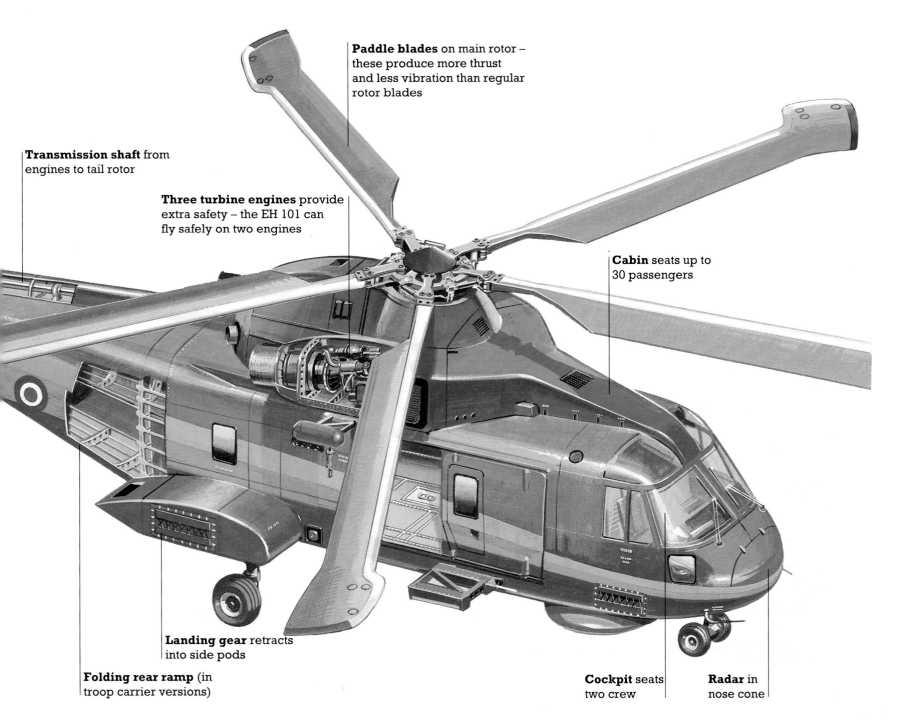

Paddle blades on main rotor – these produce more thrust and less vibration than regular rotor blades

Transmission shaft from engines to tail rotor

Three turbine engines provide extra safety – the EH 101 can fly safely on two engines

Cabin seats up to 30 passengers

Landing gear retracts into side pods

Folding rear ramp (in troop carrier versions)

Cockpit seats two crew

Radar in nose cone

The first helicopters

The great Italian artist and engineer Leonardo da Vinci designed a kind of helicopter nearly 500 years ago. His idea is illustrated below. But it was not until 1907 that the first person-carrying helicopter left the ground under its own power. This was a machine built by French inventor Paul Cornu. He called it a "flying bicycle."

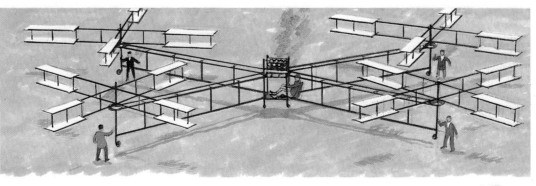

▽ Da Vinci's "helicopter" was designed to screw up into the air. The word *helicopter* comes from two Greek words, *helix* (spiral) and *pteron* (wing).

▷ The Gyroplane No.1 (top) beat Cornu's machine into the air by a few months. But this complex machine had to be steadied by helpers, so it was not a free flight.
  Cornu's "flying bicycle" (right) was the first successful rotary-winged aircraft.

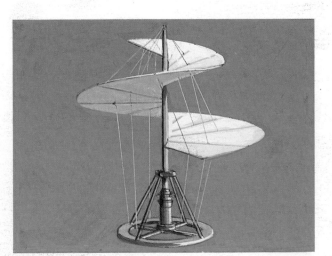

◁ Russian designer Igor Sikorsky settled in the United States, where he built the VS-300, the first helicopter to use a tail rotor successfully to control its direction. He is shown here in 1939, lifting the tethered machine off the ground.

▷ The VS-300 in 1941, streamlined and fitted with floats for water takeoffs.

Front rotor

Leather drive belts connect rotors to engine

Small gasoline engine

Bicycle wheels

Rear rotor

Flying a helicopter

Flying a helicopter is more difficult than flying a regular fixed-wing aircraft. A helicopter can easily spin out of control.

As well as traveling forward, helicopters are designed to fly backward, sideways, up or down, and to hover motionless. The pilot must be able to handle several controls at once.

◁ This helicopter cockpit has two sets of controls, with one for the pilot and one for the co-pilot. The foot pedals work the tail rotor, which controls the direction in which the helicopter points. The stick between the seats is called the collective pitch lever. It has a twist-grip for controlling engine power. Pulling up on the collective lever provides lift. Lowering it reduces lift so that the helicopter hovers or descends. The pilots use the curved levers, or control columns, to produce forward, backward, or sideways flight.

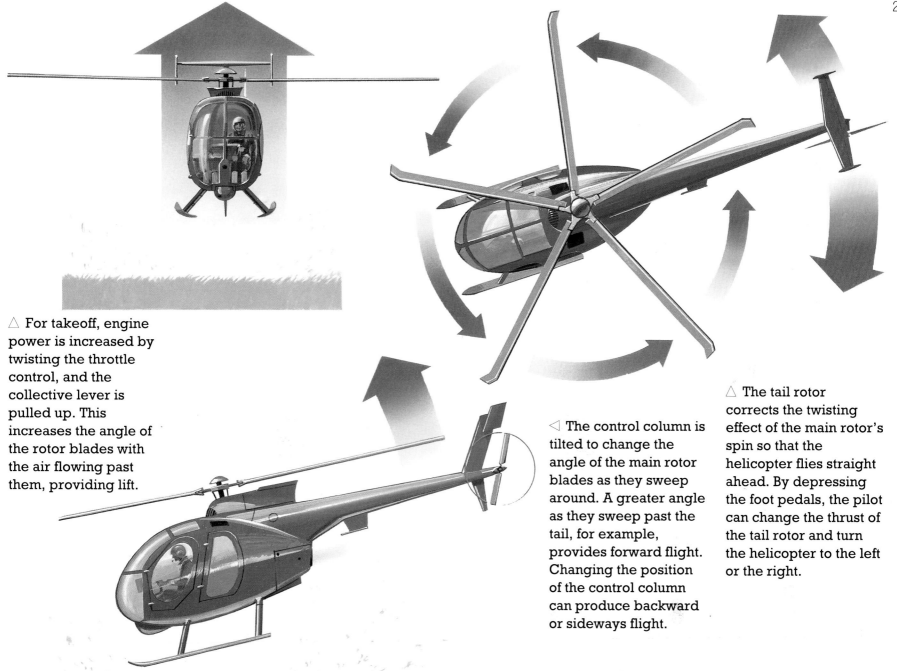

△ For takeoff, engine power is increased by twisting the throttle control, and the collective lever is pulled up. This increases the angle of the rotor blades with the air flowing past them, providing lift.

◁ The control column is tilted to change the angle of the main rotor blades as they sweep around. A greater angle as they sweep past the tail, for example, provides forward flight. Changing the position of the control column can produce backward or sideways flight.

△ The tail rotor corrects the twisting effect of the main rotor's spin so that the helicopter flies straight ahead. By depressing the foot pedals, the pilot can change the thrust of the tail rotor and turn the helicopter to the left or the right.

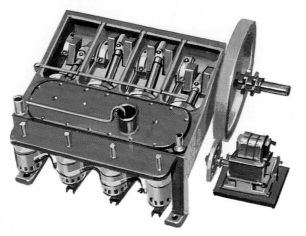

◁ The Wrights built their own gasoline engine for the *Flyer* as no automobile engine was light enough. The control system they used was the result of several years of experiments with gliders.

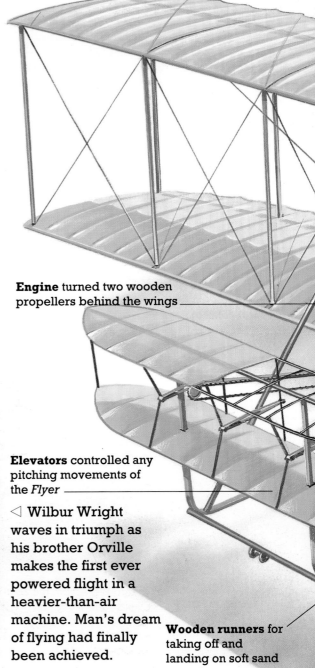

Engine turned two wooden propellers behind the wings

Elevators controlled any pitching movements of the *Flyer*

◁ Wilbur Wright waves in triumph as his brother Orville makes the first ever powered flight in a heavier-than-air machine. Man's dream of flying had finally been achieved.

Wooden runners for taking off and landing on soft sand

The Wright Flyer

The great age of aviation began one December morning in 1903 on a beach near Kitty Hawk in the state of North Carolina. The Wright *Flyer*, built mainly of wood and fabric by the brothers Wilbur and Orville Wright, took to the air and stayed aloft for 12 seconds.

Bicycle-type chains
linked engine to propellers

Radiator

Propeller

Fuel tank

Twin rudders

Propeller

Wing-warping wire

Wing ribs
made of ash

Cradle around pilot's hips attached by wires and pulleys to wing tips – by moving his hips, he could twist one wing tip or the other to maintain balance in flight

Pilot, lying across the middle of the lower wing, moved his body from side to side to control the plane in banking maneuvers

Wings, each measuring 40 feet 4 inches (12.29 m) from tip to tip, were wooden frames covered with a cotton fabric.

Elevator control

Bracing struts
made of spruce

Early designs

The early years of aviation, both before and after the Wright *Flyer*, were a time of great experimentation. There were no rules to say where wings, engines, fins, or rudders should be. Nor were there any standards governing the number or shape of these elements of an aircraft.

Some of the early flying machines are illustrated here, drawn to the same scale.

△ Triplane glider of 1849, built by Sir George Cayley (UK). Cayley realized that a powerful engine was needed for successful flight. But only cumbersome steam engines were available in his time.

▽ Steam-powered craft of Félix du Temple (France) was the first powered aircraft to leave the ground, in 1874, but only for a few moments down a slope.

▷ The bat-winged craft of Clément Ader (France) chugged into the air in 1890 for a short distance but only just off the ground and without any steering controls.

△ The Wright *Flyer* (USA), the first successful powered flying machine (1903).

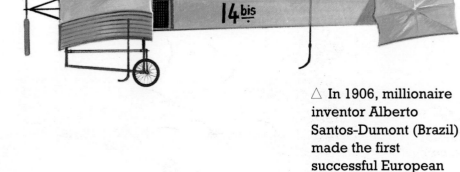

△ In 1906, millionaire inventor Alberto Santos-Dumont (Brazil) made the first successful European flights in his *14-bis*.

▽ The Wright Brothers made another great advance in aviation with their *Type A* (1908). Its flight controls enabled the pilot to roll, bank, and turn the plane.

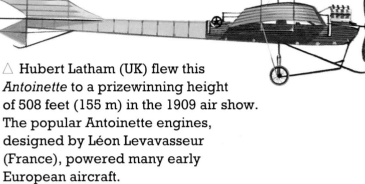

△ The *Golden Flyer*, flown by Glenn Curtiss (USA), won speed prizes in the world's first air show, in France in 1909.

▽ The *Blériot XI*, in which Louis Blériot (France) made the first successful crossing of the English Channel, on July 25, 1909.

△ Hubert Latham (UK) flew this *Antoinette* to a prizewinning height of 508 feet (155 m) in the 1909 air show. The popular Antoinette engines, designed by Léon Levavasseur (France), powered many early European aircraft.

△ The Morane Saulnier monoplane in which Roland Garros (France) crossed the Mediterranean non-stop in 1913.

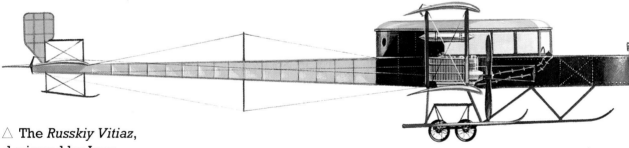

△ The *Russkiy Vitiaz*, designed by Igor Sikorsky (Russia) of later helicopter fame, flew in 1913. With four engines, it was the first successful big aircraft.

▷ In the 1970s designers reverted to some of the early ideas to achieve the first man-powered flight. In 1979, professional cyclist Bryan Allen (UK) pedaled the *Gossamer Albatross* across the English Channel.

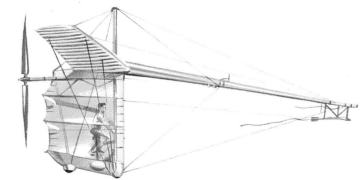

Long-distance flyers

The 1920s and 1930s were a period of great adventure, with pioneering pilots flying long distances across the world.

Among these were Charles Lindbergh, who made the first solo flight across the Atlantic, Richard Byrd, the first to fly over the South Pole, and Amy Johnson, who flew solo from England to Australia

▽ The *Spirit of St. Louis* at the end of its epic flight, as American airmail pilot Charles Lindbergh prepares to land at Le Bourget airport, near Paris. The 3,610-mile (5,810 km) trip from New York took 33 hours 29 minutes. During the long transatlantic journey Lindbergh had to fight to keep awake before he landed in France to a hero's welcome.

▽ The two planes below are typical of the machines used on record-breaking flights and also represent old and new technologies. On the left is the light biplane flown by British aviator Amy Johnson, when she became the first woman to fly solo from England to Australia. On the right is the heavier, multi-engined monoplane flown by American explorer Richard Byrd over the South Pole.

Framework, mostly of wood covered with stretched, painted fabric

Single-seat cockpit

Single wing with metal skin

▽ **Ford 4-AT Tri-motor**

Enclosed cockpit

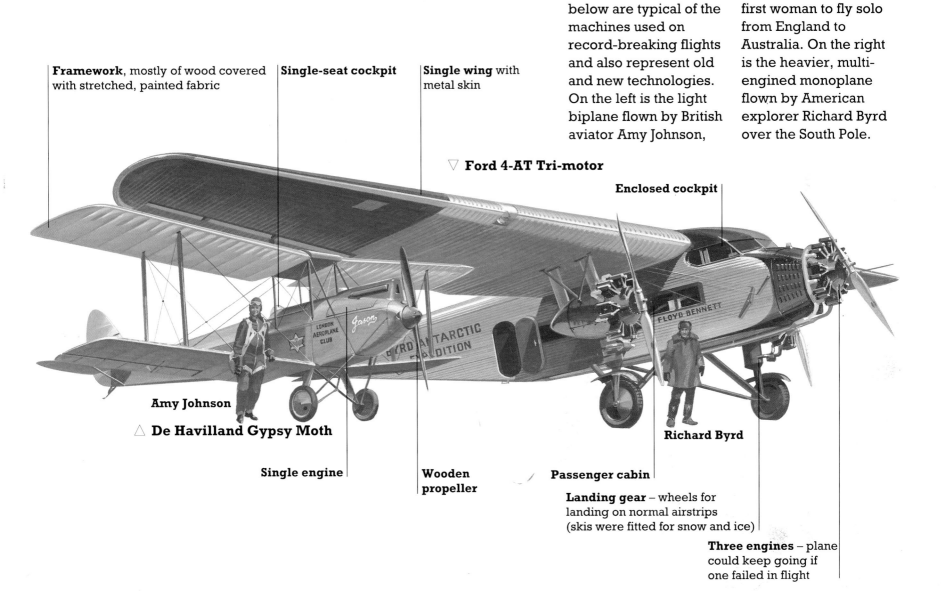

Amy Johnson

△ **De Havilland Gypsy Moth**

Richard Byrd

Single engine

Wooden propeller

Passenger cabin

Landing gear – wheels for landing on normal airstrips (skis were fitted for snow and ice)

Three engines – plane could keep going if one failed in flight

Rocket plane

The North American X-15 rocket plane blazed a high-speed trail through the skies in the 1960s. Three X-15s were built, making 199 flights between them. Test pilot William Knight flew the last mission. On October 3, 1967, after just over two minutes of rocket burn, the X-15 reached a speed of 4,520 mph (7,274 km/h). This was a world record, which still stands as the fastest winged flight ever.

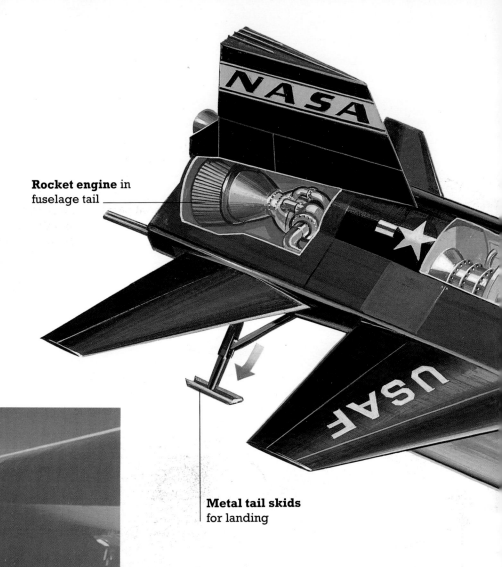

Rocket engine in fuselage tail

Metal tail skids for landing

◁ An X-15 tucked under the starboard wing of a giant B-52 Stratofortress. The X-15s were taken up by these modified bombers and launched in midair for their experimental flights.

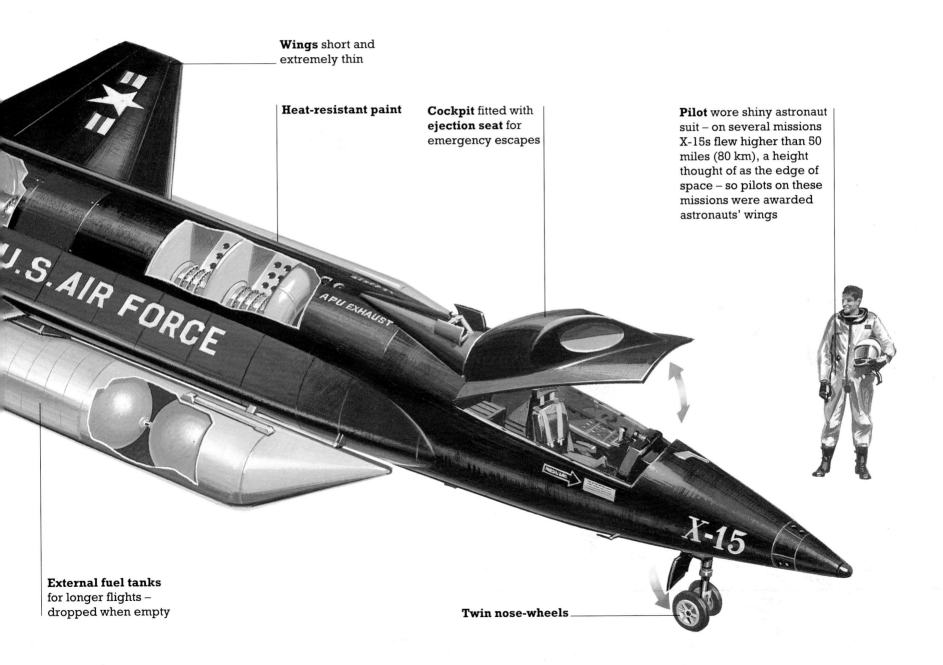

Wings short and extremely thin

Heat-resistant paint

Cockpit fitted with **ejection seat** for emergency escapes

Pilot wore shiny astronaut suit – on several missions X-15s flew higher than 50 miles (80 km), a height thought of as the edge of space – so pilots on these missions were awarded astronauts' wings

U.S. AIR FORCE

APU EXHAUST

X-15

External fuel tanks for longer flights – dropped when empty

Twin nose-wheels

Epic flights

The craft on these pages all made their mark on the history of flying. It began with the Montgolfier balloon in 1783. Since then, all kinds of craft – airships and planes – have been involved in epic flights.

The Wright *Flyer* and other record-breaking aircraft have been illustrated on previous pages. The history makers on the opposite page are drawn approximately to the same scale

◁ The first aerial voyages in history took place over Paris in 1783, when balloons designed by the Montgolfier brothers Joseph and Étienne, made the first manned and untethered flights.

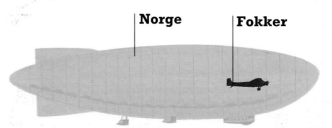

Norge   **Fokker**

△ In 1926, two contrasting craft took part in a friendly contest to be the first to fly over the North Pole. Richard Byrd's American team with a three-engined Fokker plane were the first to make it. Two days later, an Italian team in a huge airship, the *Norge*, also flew over the Pole.

◁ Douglas World Cruiser (USA) made the first around-the-world flight, April 6 to September 28, 1924.

△▽ *Voyager* (USA) was an aircraft built for one special mission – around the world, non-stop and without refueling. The pilots, Dick Rutan and Jeana Yeager, did it in nine days in 1986.

△ The *Spirit of St. Louis*, flown by Charles Lindbergh (USA) on his solo transatlantic flight in 1927.

▽ *Winnie Mae*, the Lockheed Vega flown by Wiley Post (USA) in July 1933 on the first solo flight around the world.

△ The converted Vickers Vimy bomber flown by John Alcock and Arthur Brown (UK) in June 1919 on the first nonstop transatlantic flight.

▽ A Curtiss NC-4 flying boat (USA) was the first plane to cross the Atlantic. It flew from Newfoundland to Portugal in May 1919, refueling on the Azores islands.

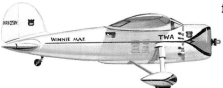

Hot-air balloon

Drifting in the breeze in a hot-air balloon is a leisurely way to travel. People do not use balloons to get from place to place, but to enjoy the thrill of floating quietly over beautiful countryside. The silence is broken only by bursts of the burner to reheat the air.

The main principle of ballooning is that hot air rises. The pilot cannot steer a balloon in the normal way, but changes height to find new wind directions.

◁ The people and passengers travel in a basket suspended from the envelope, or bag – the part that encloses the air. This is usually brightly colored and many balloons bear the name of a sponsor.

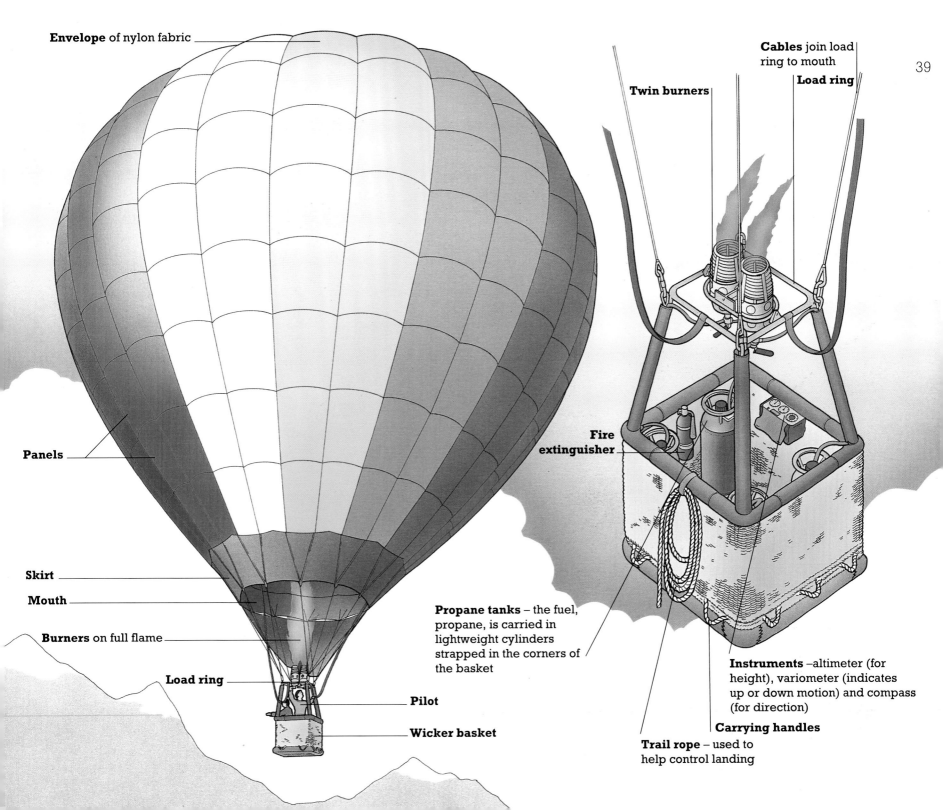

Envelope of nylon fabric

Cables join load ring to mouth

Load ring

Twin burners

Panels

Fire extinguisher

Skirt

Mouth

Burners on full flame

Propane tanks – the fuel, propane, is carried in lightweight cylinders strapped in the corners of the basket

Load ring

Pilot

Wicker basket

Instruments –altimeter (for height), variometer (indicates up or down motion) and compass (for direction)

Carrying handles

Trail rope – used to help control landing

Airship

Airships, like balloons, are lighter than air, but they are powered by engines and can be steered. The large body of an airship, the envelope, contains a lighter-than-air gas. This lifts the craft and keeps it aloft. The engines move it through the air.

The age of passenger airships reached its height in the 1930s. These were "rigid" – they had a light metal framework. Today's airships are non-rigid. They are known as "blimps." They are used mainly for advertising or as airborne platforms for television cameras.

◁ A hot-air airship is used to carry advertising – a kind of flying billboard. These craft have burners, like a hot-air balloon, but can be driven and steered. The pilot sits in a gondola under the envelope.

▷ Non-rigid airships are again being designed and built for carrying passengers. They may also come into use as a cheap method of carrying cargo. (Drawing based on Advanced Airship Corporation design)

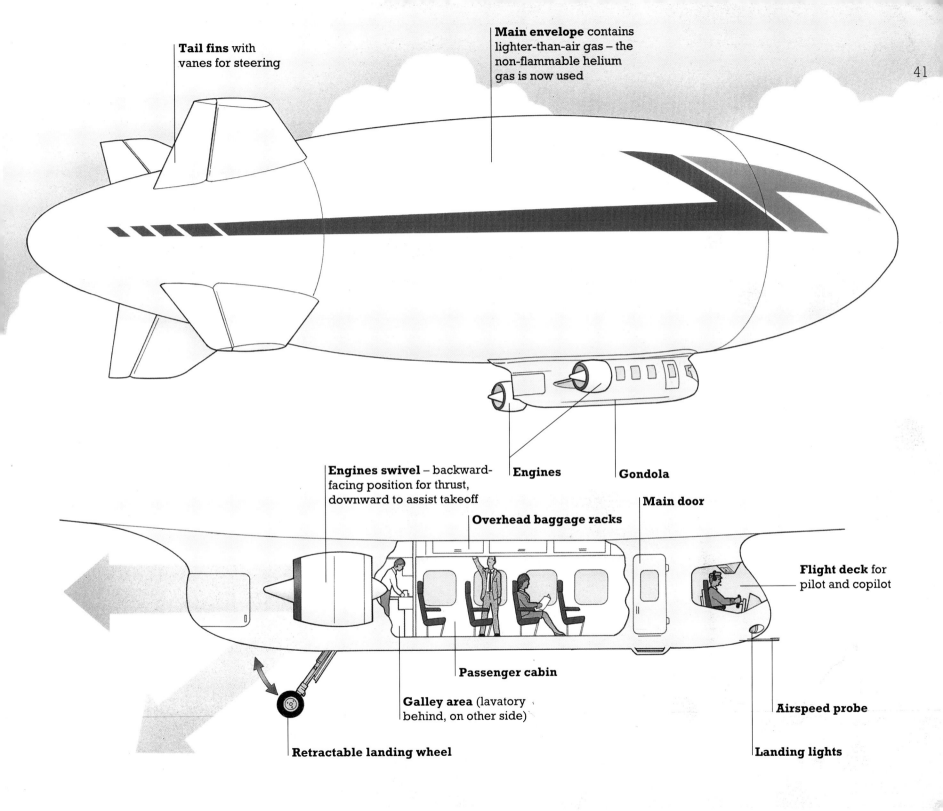

Tail fins with vanes for steering

Main envelope contains lighter-than-air gas – the non-flammable helium gas is now used

Engines

Gondola

Engines swivel – backward-facing position for thrust, downward to assist takeoff

Overhead baggage racks

Main door

Flight deck for pilot and copilot

Passenger cabin

Galley area (lavatory behind, on other side)

Retractable landing wheel

Airspeed probe

Landing lights

Space shuttle

Space shuttles fly people out of the earth's atmosphere and into space. The shuttle lifts off like a rocket, travels like a spacecraft and lands back on earth like a plane.

Shuttles are the first reusable spacecraft. Their uses include launching satellites and carrying out experiments in space.

NASA developed the space shuttle and began flying missions from the United States in 1981. Other shuttles are being developed by the European Space Agency.

External fuel tank carries fuel for orbiter's liftoff engines. It is released when empty and falls into the sea.

◁ A shuttle orbits the earth. The photograph was taken by a satellite temporarily placed into orbit.

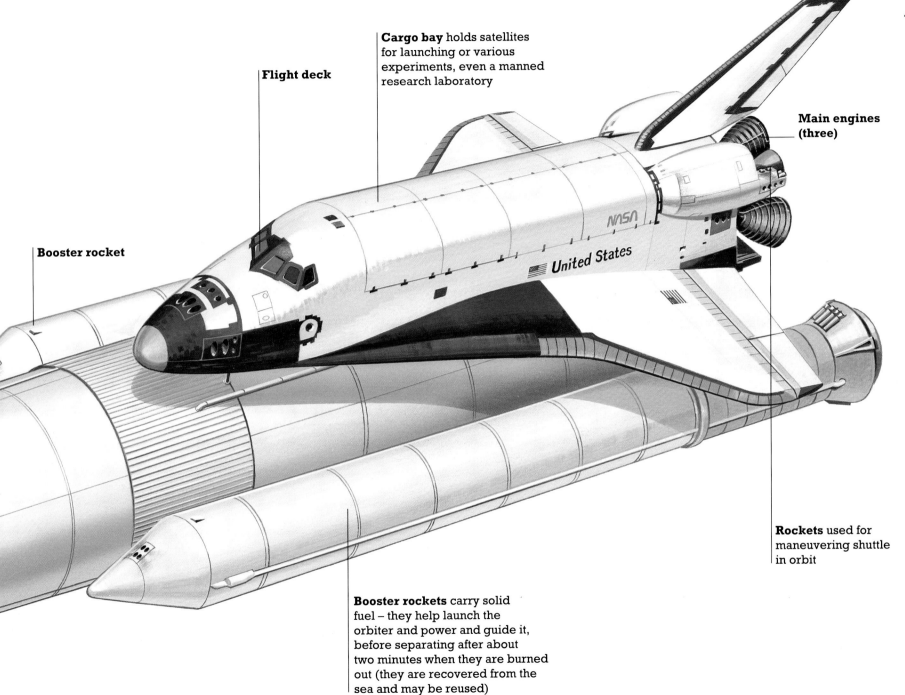

Cargo bay holds satellites for launching or various experiments, even a manned research laboratory

Flight deck

Main engines (three)

Booster rocket

Rockets used for maneuvering shuttle in orbit

Booster rockets carry solid fuel – they help launch the orbiter and power and guide it, before separating after about two minutes when they are burned out (they are recovered from the sea and may be reused)

NASA

United States

Famous firsts

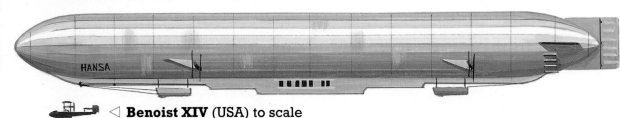

◁ **Benoist XIV** (USA) to scale

△ The *Hansa* airship and the Benoist XIV flying boat provided the world's first air passenger services.

The first airlines

The first regular passenger flights were in airships of the German Delag company, which operated from June 1910 until August 1914, despite several losses through storms, fires, and engine failure.

The first airline service to use planes was the St. Petersburg and Tampa Airboat Line, in Florida, from January 1 to late April 1914. It operated a Benoist Type XIV flying boat carrying a single passenger.

The first turboprop

Turboprop planes use jet engines to turn propellers. They are quiet and economical, and popular for shorter journeys. The 1953 Vickers Viscount was the first turboprop airliner.

▽ **Vickers Viscount** (UK)

The first jetliner

The De Havilland Comet was the first airliner to have jet engines. It first flew in 1949, and BOAC began operating the world's first jet passenger service in 1952.

△ **De Havilland Comet** (UK)

High-altitude flight

Boeing Stratoliner (USA)

Before World War II, airliners flew at quite low altitudes. But most storms occur here, too. Airline companies realized that they would have to fly at higher altitudes, above the weather, to give their passengers a smoother ride. But there is not enough oxygen at high altitude.

Designers got to work and produced the Boeing Stratoliner, the first airliner to operate at high altitudes. It had a sealed cabin, with pumps to keep the air pressure inside at that of an altitude of 12,000 feet (3,660 m), even when the plane was cruising at 23,000 feet (7,100 m).

Supersonic flight

The first aircraft to break the sound barrier was the Bell X-1 piloted by Charles Yeager.

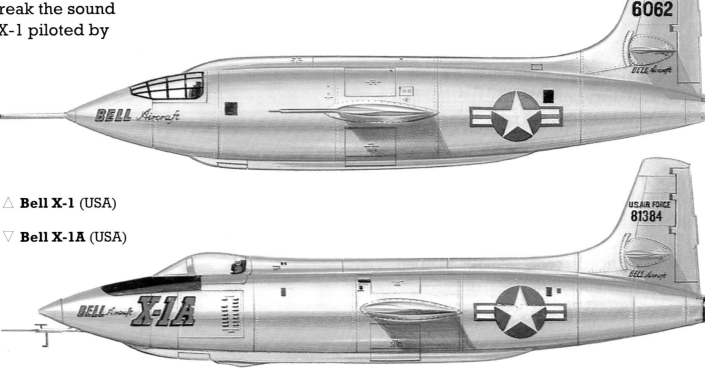

△ **Bell X-1** (USA)

▽ **Bell X-1A** (USA)

▷ The Bell X-1 rocket plane was specially designed with thin wings and a high-set tail. This was to avoid the shock-wave problems that had previously killed pilots attempting to fly faster than the speed of sound. On October 14, 1947, pilot Charles Yeager flew it at Mach 1.015 (1.015 times the speed of sound). He later flew the Bell X-1A at faster speeds.

△ The X-15 broke all records, with speeds approaching Mach 7. X-15s came in for glider landings, unused rocket fuel being dumped at altitude.

Jumbo jet

The mighty Boeing 747 – the jumbo jet – was the first airliner to carry more than 500 passengers. It first flew in 1969, and one version carried a record 610 passengers in 1981.

The 747-300 version can seat 516 in the main cabin plus 69 in the upper deck. The newer 747-400 has a capacity for only about 420 passengers.

△ The Boeing 747 (USA), or "jumbo jet," was the world's first wide-bodied airliner.

Odds and ends

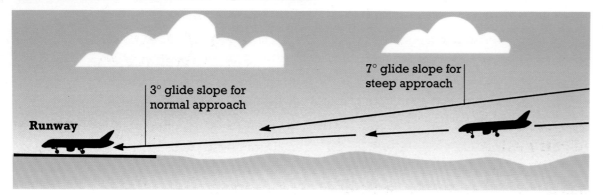

3° glide slope for normal approach

7° glide slope for steep approach

Runway

△ The diagram shows the glide slope for a normal approach and one for a steeper landing.

▽ The BAe 146 (UK), the world's quietest jet airliner.

Quietest jet

The British Aerospace 146 is a short-haul airliner carrying about 90 passengers. It is not a big plane but has four turbofan engines slung under its high-mounted wings. The engines are so quiet that the plane can make night flights to airports that normally ban jets after dark because of the noise they make.

Approach and landing

The path an airliner follows on its approach to an airport is called the glide slope. For a normal approach, this is at 3 degrees to the runway.

Best-selling jet

The twin-engined 737 is the baby of the Boeing jetliner family. In 1987 it outsold Boeing's other best-seller, the 727, to become the most widely ordered jet ever, with well over 2,000 planes bought.

△ **Boeing 737 (USA)**

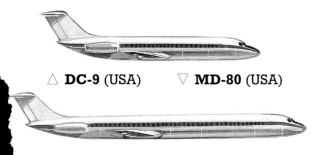

△ **DC-9** (USA)   ▽ **MD-80** (USA)

Most stretched jet

Some airliners have been redesigned to accommodate more passengers. This is known as stretching. The most stretched jet is the McDonnell Douglas MD-80. It started off in 1965 as the DC-9, a 90-seater measuring 104 feet (31.82 m) in length. After several stretches, the MD-80 measures 148 feet (45.06 m) and carries 179 passengers.

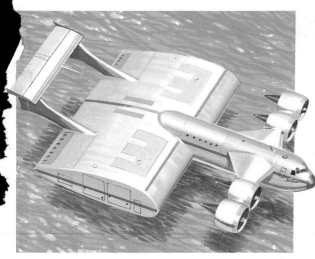

△ An idea from Lockheed (USA) for a giant airlifter of the 21st century.

Future airlifters

There are plans for making airliners even bigger, for carrying more passengers or freight. A French company, Hydro 2000, has a project for a massive seaplane able to carry a 270-ton (300 t) load – or more than 4,000 people. Lockheed has designed an airlifter with an enormous wing for carrying the cargo.

Flying upside down

Stunt flying is an exciting feature of air shows. Aircraft perform solo or in teams. Flying upside down is not something that can be done in any plane. Aircraft used in displays have special fuel systems that can cope with maneuvers that turn the plane over.

▽ Flying upside down, a basic maneuver in displays.